LIGHTNING BOLT BOOKS™

The Monarch Butterfly's Journey

Jon M. Fishman

Lerner Publications • Minneapolis

For my mom, a monarch fan

Lerner Publications Company
A division of Lerner Publishing Group, Inc.
241 First Avenue North
Minneapolis, MN 55401 USA

For reading levels and more information, look up this title at www.lernerbooks.com.

Library of Congress Cataloging-in-Publication Data

Names: Fishman, Jon M., author.
Title: The monarch butterfly's journey / Jon M. Fishman.
Description: Minneapolis : Lerner Publications, [2018] | Series: Lightning bolt books. Amazing migrators | Includes bibliographical references and index. | Audience: Age 6-9. | Audience: K to Grade 3.
Identifiers: LCCN 2017005928 (print) | LCCN 2017008470 (ebook) | ISBN 9781512486339 (lb : alk. paper) | ISBN 9781512498110 (eb pdf)
Subjects: LCSH: Monarch butterfly—Juvenile literature.
Classification: LCC QL561.D3 F57 2018 (print) | LCC QL561.D3 (ebook) | DDC 595.78/9—dc23

LC record available at https://lccn.loc.gov/2017005928

Manufactured in the United States of America
1-43457-33197-4/28/2017

Table of Contents

Meet the Monarch Butterfly 4

A Monarch Caterpillar Hatches 8

A Monarch Butterfly Migrates 12

Monarch Butterflies in Danger 16

Fun Facts 20

More Amazing Migrators 21

Glossary 22

Further Reading 23

Index 24

Meet the Monarch Butterfly

A monarch butterfly flaps its orange and black wings. The monarch lands on the edge of a flower. Monarchs pollinate flowers.

Pollinating is the process of moving pollen from flower to flower. It helps flowers grow.

The butterfly grips the flower with its four back legs. Its two front legs are small and close to the body. The monarch drinks nectar from the flower.

Monarch butterflies use nectar as fuel for their long journey. They are migrators. They move from one area to another at different times of the year.

The monarch soars to a new flower. Soon the butterfly will begin a journey that may take it thousands of miles away.

The monarch uses its four wings to fly.

A Monarch Caterpillar Hatches

A female monarch butterfly lands on a milkweed plant. She looks for a good place to lay an egg. Then she lays a sticky egg on the bottom of a leaf.

Monarchs lay eggs only on milkweed plants.

A monarch caterpillar is about the size of a grain of rice when it hatches.

A monarch may lay hundreds of eggs. A white caterpillar hatches from each egg in about four days. It eats the eggshell and the milkweed leaf.

The caterpillar eats and grows.
It sheds its skin four times.
Each time it becomes larger
and more colorful.

Molting is the name for
what a caterpillar does
when it sheds its skin.

The caterpillar hangs upside down from a milkweed plant. It sheds again and forms a hard shell called a chrysalis. A monarch butterfly comes out of its chrysalis after about two weeks.

A Monarch Butterfly Migrates

Most monarchs live in the United States and Canada during the summer. But those places are too cold for butterflies in the winter. Monarchs migrate south so they can survive.

Some monarchs travel 3,000 miles (4,828 km) when they migrate!

A monarch butterfly soars on a warm breeze. It turns toward a bright flower. Monarchs stop to eat as they travel.

Monarchs that live west of the Rocky Mountains migrate to California for the winter. Monarchs from east of the mountains go to Mexico.

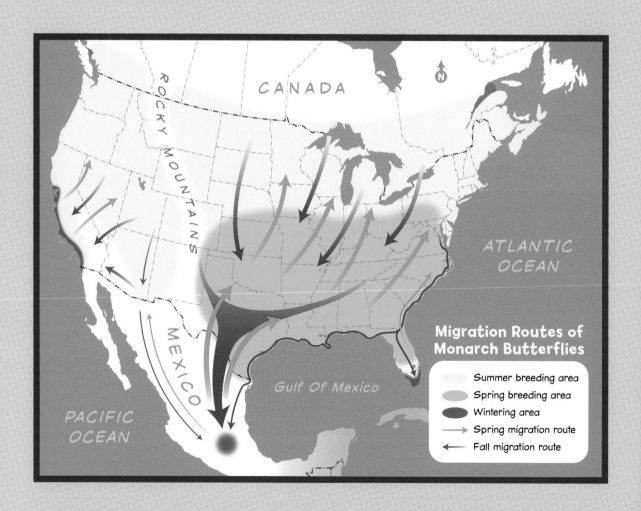

Migration Routes of Monarch Butterflies

- Summer breeding area
- Spring breeding area
- Wintering area
- → Spring migration route
- ← Fall migration route

At night, monarchs rest together in trees. This tree is full of butterflies!

Millions of monarchs flap and float. It is spring, and they are heading north. They lay eggs and drink nectar along the way.

Monarch Butterflies in Danger

Bzzz! What is that sound? It is a wasp! The wasp stings a monarch butterfly caterpillar.

Animals such as wasps and ants hunt caterpillars and their eggs for food.

Humans are an even bigger danger to monarchs than wasps. People build homes where monarchs live. They tear down trees and take out flowers. Farmers spray poison in their fields to get rid of milkweed plants.

Humans have taken away many of the plants along the monarchs' migration path.

Monarchs need to rest on trees. If they don't have enough milkweed or flowers to eat, they cannot live.

But humans can help monarchs too! Students plant milkweed in a butterfly garden. Monarchs will lay eggs on the milkweed. Then they will continue their long journey.

Fun Facts

- Monarch caterpillars eat as much as they can. They can eat a milkweed leaf in just minutes. They even eat their own skin after shedding it!

- Monarchs don't move much in the winter. They stay in trees and move only on the warmest days to drink nectar.

- A monarch butterfly uses the sun as a guide when it migrates. This is one of the reasons monarchs travel only during the day.

More Amazing Migrators

- Monarchs are not the only butterflies that migrate. The painted lady butterfly travels from Africa all the way to Europe.

- Scientists think that less than 25 percent of birds in Canada stay there for the winter. But the planet is getting warmer. More birds are staying in Canada all year as temperatures rise.

- A lot of other insects migrate. Moths, dragonflies, and locusts travel with the seasons.

Glossary

caterpillar: a wormlike creature that hatches from an egg

chrysalis: a hard shell that covers a caterpillar as it changes into a butterfly

migrator: an animal that moves from one area to another at different times of the year

milkweed: a plant with milky juice

nectar: a sweet liquid from plants

pollinate: to help plants spread by moving pollen from one plant to another plant of the same kind

shed: to remove something such as skin

Further Reading

Boothroyd, Jennifer. *Let's Visit the Grassland*. Minneapolis: Lerner Publications, 2017.

Ducksters: Animal Migrations
http://www.ducksters.com/animals/animal_migrations.php

Gregory, Josh. *Monarch Butterflies*. New York: Children's Press, 2016.

Hirsch, Rebecca E. *Thousand-Mile Fliers and Other Amazing Migrators*. Minneapolis: Lerner Publications, 2017.

Kidzone: The Monarch Butterfly
http://www.kidzone.ws/animals/monarch_butterfly.htm

National Geographic Kids: Monarch Butterfly
http://kids.nationalgeographic.com/animals/monarch-butterfly/#monarch-butterfly-grass.jpg

Index

caterpillar, 9-11, 16

chrysalis, 11

egg, 8-9, 15, 19

food, 9-10, 18

migrate, 6, 12, 14

milkweed, 8-9, 11, 17-19

pollinate, 4

wings, 4

Photo Acknowledgments

The images in this book are used with the permission of: © Howard Cheek/ Dreamstime.com, p. 2; © Tracyevansphotography/Dreamstime.com, p. 4; © Marilyn Gould/ Dreamstime.com, p. 5; JHVEPhoto/Shutterstock.com, p. 6; © Henmand/Dreamstime.com, pp. 7, 18, 20; © iStockphoto.com/ParkerDeen, p. 8; Cathy Keifer/Shutterstock.com, p. 9; © iStockphoto.com/dossyl, p. 10; © Dml231/Dreamstime.com, p. 11; © iStockphoto.com/ cicloco, p. 12; © Brian Kushner/Dreamstime.com, p. 13; © Laura Westlund/Independent Picture Service, p. 14; © iStockphoto.com/Spondylolithesis, p. 15; © iStockphoto.com/ johnandersonphoto, p. 16; Dick Kenny/Shutterstock.com, p. 17; © iStockphoto.com/asiseeit, p. 19; © iStockphoto.com/Walkingby, p. 22.

Front cover: © Chris Austin/Dreamstime.com.

Main body text set in Billy Infant regular 28/36. Typeface provided by SparkType.